HARNESSING DARKNESS

Expressing Mental Illness Through Poetry

CALEB WOODS

Cover and Book Design by Luke Johnson

Photographs of the Author © Luke Johnson

ISBN: 978-0-578-53146-5

To anyone who has been affected by mental illness in any way, shape, or form, this book is dedicated to you.

AUTHOR'S NOTE

The poems you're about to read come from my very essence.
They flowed through me onto paper during moments of trauma,
hardship, anxiety, and depression. My hope is that those suffering
from mental illness will feel comforted knowing they're not alone
after reading the poetry I've written.

These personal, deep, and thought-provoking poems are a
product of my ability to cope with my mental illness. I have
struggled with anxiety and depression my entire life. Since being
diagnosed with PTSD, I've managed to find solace through
writing.

The poems you're about to read are heavy. Some touch on
difficult subjects while others add a bit of hope. For those who've
had the luxury of never suffering from any type of mental illness,
I hope these poems are able to show you what it's like for
someone who struggles with all the symptoms PTSD brings –
night terrors, panic attacks, flashbacks, suicidal ideations, etc.

Thank you for taking the time to learn about this part of me. I
appreciate you more than I can say.

CONTENTS

It seems as if the existential question you wrestle with is, "If I'm not loved, do I exist?"

–Dr. Sullivan (my psychologist)

BIRTH

Killing Myself with Words

I slit my wrists to let the words come out.
It drains me dry, but here they are, written for you.

Who am I kidding? These words are for me.
I don't breathe air. I breathe words.

Words, words, words,
flowing out of me onto the page.

It's as if my blood is ink,
pooling in my body until I release it.

I suffer through the pain as the words flow out of me,
barely surviving each time.

The Bottom

Jump in, the water's fine.
It's nice and clear.
A little cloudy perhaps,
but you can still see.

Can you touch the bottom?
Could you if you tried?
The bottom's a scary place to be,
but you have a better grip there.

There's nowhere to hold up here.
The bottom is firm, always present.
It doesn't change like
the water up here does.

Drown. Drown. Drown.
Sink.
Bubbles.

The tiny bubbles float out,
like little moments of your life.
One last chance to leave
your mark on the world.

Pop. Pop. Pop.
Gone as they reach the surface.

Travel lower and lower.
Deep breaths
of ocean, of sea,
of everything in-between.

Swallowed, but finally whole.
Thirsty, but full.

It's solid at the bottom,
concrete and permanent.
No waves.
Just stillness, quiet.

Pop.

Flying

Your wings carry me across the void.
Looking down, I see total darkness.
You tell me you see sky below us.
Maybe my view is distorted.
At least I'm safe with you.

But when will I grow wings of my own?
I've tried to fly before, but always fail.
Clipped wings suit me so well.
Stopped in my tracks
by forces beyond my control.

Growing new wings takes work –
lots of effort when I have no energy left.
Using the wings I have? That's the key –
making something broken new again.
A bandage helps, but scars remain.

To some, flying is easy,
sailing away, up and over,
in-between clouds of wonder.
I'm still trying to navigate the ground.
It has this strong hold on me.

Like chains weighing me down,
I'm trapped as feathers are plucked.
The weight comes from up above as well.
The world weighing on my shoulders –
that's how my wings were clipped.

Locked Inside

Up and down the stairs, room to room,
constantly locking doors and windows
in this hollow house.

Am I alone? Was I ever?
There's a different sound.
I'm off again.

It's flight today,
fight tomorrow.
Always the same routine.

Another loud noise –
the race begins again.
Can't ever catch up, can't ever win.

Coming Alive

The birth begins long before
we become alive.
It isn't until reality sets in
when we take our first breath.

The cold, stark realization –
the full range of human emotions.
Pain. Anger. Loss.
Experiences that alter us.

Changing our reality
into something abnormal and abstract.
Forever different,
we see our surroundings.

What once was a cornucopia of color
fades to darkness.
An ever-present stillness
brings a hush over the world.

We dissolve into the black,
losing shades of us,
of each other,
along the way.

Coping to Survive

The gnawing noise wreaks havoc,
scratching, screeching.
My distracted brain makes tiny footnotes.

Like a court reporter
documenting each tragedy
to compile for my mind.

My Santa Claus list is getting longer
as the notes pile up.
Surrounded by paper –

weaving in, about, and around me
like the muscles of the brain.
We are our own organism.

Our coping mechanisms keep us alive,
helping us hold on to fragments.
A part of us, apart from us.

These tiny mechanisms cling to us –
attract like a magnet,
then dissolve.

Coping is only surviving.
To truly live,
we must accept our lives as they are.

But we keep crafting.
Crafting our mechanisms, crafting our stories.
Always the artists, we are.

Everywhere I'm Not

You don't know what it's like to be broken,
to feel like the pieces of you
are scattered across the earth.
Not physically, but in time.

Pieces stuck in the past,
where you can never reach.
You can't get them back,
no matter how hard you try.

A sliver of me remains
in the classrooms
of my elementary school
where I was first tormented.

Another piece of me
haunts the hallways
of my high school
where the harassment took place.

A large part of me
lies on the floor of
my rapist's apartment.
Stuck in the fibers of the carpet,
destined to always be stepped on.

I left two pieces of me
at separate funeral homes.
One for you, one for me.
Both times, a severed tie.

Cut up in tiny little pieces,
fed to the world.
Shattering my whole self.
Crumbs of a life.

Giving it All

I feel out of control,
like I'm no longer in charge of my body.

My mind isn't connected to me,
it tells me things to do, what to say.

It wants me to kill myself.
I'm not sure I disagree.

It wants me to get up, right now,
and find the sharpest object in the room.

Why does it want me gone?
I must be too powerful to be kept alive.

This is my only thought.
Maybe that's why I should stay.

The world should fear me and what I can do.
It should watch out.

Here I come,
giving you my life.

Not Good Enough

The books on the shelf mock me.
They look at me smugly,
knowing it's difficult for me to simply get up off the couch.

These invisible stories appeal to me – the covers, the synopses.
But they're better than anything I can do.
And they know it.

They're a tease, staring at me with their awards and prizes.
My words will never amount to their weight.
I wish.

It would be nice for people to know my story –
to write my book perfectly, adding everything you need to know.
But it's impossible.

I just don't have it in me.
The time, the effort,
the soul it takes to bear and reveal so, so many secrets.

It's a heartbreaking affair that tears you apart
from the inside
until you're but nothing.

In the end,
only the novel remains.
And I'm left, of course, insane.

Ash on the floor.
Burnt up from spending all my energy.
The only energy I ever had to give.

Shades

Fading fast,
like using a pencil to shade.

Those quick streaks of darkness,
covering up the light.

But who holds the pencil I wonder?
Is it me? Surely not.

Why would I use it to harm instead of heal?
If only there was an eraser,

a way to undo the shade, the darkness.
But this is permanent,

tattooed on the piece of paper, on me.
Showing off scars to all.

Balancing is the key,
weighing the light and the dark.

They're both permanent, important.
Just don't let one overshadow the other.

I Lost It

I swear I lost a piece of me.
I can't remember if I dropped it
or if it was pried from my grip.
Nevertheless, it's gone –

thrown into the abyss,
never to be seen again.
It would be costly
to try and find it.

It's best to just let it go,
live without it.
But what if that piece is crucial?
A significant part of who I am?

With it misplaced,
so is my existence.
Wandering about,
never knowing where to turn.

So, I settle for less,
less of myself.
Missing a piece of me,
alone with the rest.

I hold tight to the other pieces of me,
parts of my mind and soul.
I hold on to all that I can
to never forget myself.

Brainwashing

My brain betrays me –
a washing machine, constantly spinning.

Giving me unwanted thoughts,
bringing back hidden memories.

I circle the moments in my mind.
Some thoughts get more attention than others.

I try to push them back
as far as I can –

burying so much of my life
that I'm left with so little.

If only we could clean the dirty memories;
A cleanup of our lives –

leaving only the moments of joy, happiness.
But my brain just can't do that.

It spends all its time protecting me,
forcing me to relive the memories.

It wants me to go through it over and over.
It's the only way to cope –

by always analyzing,
keeping myself in a constant state of awareness.

This betrayal has ulterior motives.
What am I to trust?

Death

The sweet release of death,
how it comforts me now.
Obligations no more.
Freedom finally begins.

Like a welcomed guest in your home;
an empty house
filled with nothing and everything.

A rocking chair in the corner
where the house sitter stays,

rocking back and forth
as Death does.

LIFE

Awakened

I sit straight up in bed,
half past three.
Like a jolt of caffeine
turning my body clock on.

This internal uneasiness
springs itself on me.

I'm cursed
to feel the pain
over and over,
hour after hour,
day after day.

Time is a cruel concept,
spinning its web.

I'm trapped –
my mind travels
back and forth,
inside and out,
here and there.

Living for today,
in the present moment,
I can't.

Left out in the Cold

I wake up shivering
as if the morning dew
lay across my skin.

It's not a pretty sight –
the shakes and sweat,
the tremors.

I must've been running from you
in my dreams again.
Why don't you ever tire?

Please, just stop trying.
My body needs rest.

A thousand slumbers
to make up for all the times –
the fights and flights
and freezes.

I need that perfect temperature,
where the wind stops
for a brief moment in the afternoon
as the sun goes down.

When the slight humidity
brings me back to life.

Once a Day

Showering is a chore.
Isolated, alone –
the feelings haunt me.

Water beats on my skin.
Every drop a bullet
taking me back to the battlefield –

flashbacks and memories
to a life stolen –
stolen by rage and various emotions.

I'm confined to the shower
once a day.
The steam pulls the memories out.

I watch them, as if on a screen
until I reach for the towel
and feel its warmth.

It's all I needed
to turn me back into my regular self –
or I guess you can call it that.

Panic on The Road

I grip the steering wheel tighter as the panic sets in.

Which way do I go?
What's the best decision?
Do I go this way?
What if I made a mistake?

I drive forward,
but soon pull over.

Pulled in a million different directions,
my body freezes.
Stopped by the inevitable
            "what ifs"
that control my mind and by extension, my life.

Decisions aren't easy. They eat me alive.

Pill Popper

I name my pills after you,
each one I take represents another one of your mistakes.

I pop one pill at a time,
in the same way you took my soul – peace by peace.

I wash the pill down with water.
It's as if you're filling me with your hatred once more.

Masks

Through the peep hole
an eye presses against the glass.
I know you're there,
always watching me.

Every move I make, you see it.
You've made certain of that.
You wanted to know
and now you do.

I'm a fraud –
not the person I want to be.
And you see it.
You see all of me.

I resent you for it,
for seeing me clearly.
How dare you
not be fooled by my disguise.

Teardrops

The tears puddle up
around my eyes,
gently touching the air.

My insides shake with all their might,
forcing the tears down,
drowning myself in the process.

It's like the inhale of a cigarette,
only the smoke stays in;
as do my tears,
because I refuse to let them come out.

They'll never see the light of day
as long as it's up to me.
My hand will wipe the tears
out of sight, but not out of mind.

But the tears continue
to pool in my lungs.
I sometimes cough,
maybe shiver, or shake.

An internal earthquake
rocks me back and forth
until the tears settle
on the floor of my soul.

The Chains That Bind

My feet are caught,
trapped by the chains.

These links of metal form
a strong rope

that keeps me down,
keeps me from moving
forward.

I lift each foot upward
with all my might,

but I can't budge.
I'm still stuck,

forced to remain the same.
In the same place,
backward.

Only until I accept the weight
as a part of me

will I know the extent
of my burdens –

how far they reach,
how deep they go
inside.

I'm not simply trapped
by the chains.

They've been on so long,
we're the same.

Clung together,
forming a whole.
Ingrained.

Stuck

The quicksand pulls.
I lift my leg, but it sinks faster.
I blame myself for getting stuck
in the first place.

Woulda,
        Coulda,
                Shoulda.

Guilt.

It pools around me and latches on like a magnet.
I realize I attract, not repel.
To swim, jump, or crawl
matters not.

I'm here.
        Stuck.

Sweaty Palms

These sweaty palms
attract everything –
objects, people.
The irony is not lost on an empath.

In the end,
everything sticks.
The sticky putty of life, my palms –
holding all the power in my hands.

The power to feel.
Feeling too much
or not enough.
Either way, the feels are caught –

caught by my sweaty palms
that are always the first sign.
The anxiety comes next,
memories flood my brain.

The sweat from my palms
open the floodgates.
The tears, the thoughts
pour out of me.

I'm left breathless,
shaking and irritable.
Pissed at my palms
always betraying me.

But they're only a warning sign,
the first among many
telling me to worry,
yet reminding me I'm alive.

Contradictions

Something holds me back.
I can't put my finger on it.

Simultaneously having the urge to do
        and do not.
These invisible strings pulling me
        in opposite directions.

Purpose and Guilt
Destiny and Depression
Creation and Calamity
Activism and Pessimism
Potential and Numbness

Contradictions make me
        crazy.
If the strings were cut, would everything fall
        apart?
Or would everything compartmentalize
        itself?

Always wanting to be
        okay.
Never knowing when it will
        be.

The enjoyment of life is diminished
by the entrapment of my mind.

The Pictures

Your camera shows me smiling.
The truth can't be seen.

A picture is worth a thousand words they say,
but my lips are sealed,

sewn together –
a voiceless shell.

The pictures you take show, but don't tell.
They never reveal who I am.

Sometimes they come close, capturing a flicker of a smile here,
a pensive concentration there.

But the person you see in those photos isn't there.
He's already gone.

Blue

Blue, the color of sadness.
My favorite color.

I didn't choose it – it chose me.
All those years ago.

Drawn to all the shades.
Some happy, some not so much.

Each one, like me.
Different parts of a whole.

All parts narrowed down
to one single thing.

No one realizing
the subtle differences.

The Slices

Sitting underneath the palm tree,
I listen to the wind.
A light rustle and a cool breeze –
this place is all mine.
No outsiders are allowed in.

It's a private world,
an ocean of memories and thoughts
carving themselves into the tree
until there's nothing left
but the leaves.

The leaves cover me,
they're so big.
The slits in-between reveal slices of myself.
Maybe that's all I should ever show anyone –
the slices.

Like splices of a film strip uncovered,
putting together the pieces.
A paper shredder, that's what I am.
Corporate and boxed in.
Sliced and spliced,

longing to be back under the palm tree,
listening to the wind.
Not fazed by the rustling of leaves.
Alone and content,
my private island.

My Best Friend

Wearing the same beautiful dress
as I last saw you.
Laying there, alone,
ready for your burial.

I know it must be a dream;
you're here now.
The dark hair cascading down your shoulders,
shrouded in white.

You're walking on water
as if you're Jesus,
back to life
with newfound powers.

One hand reaches out for me,
a soft hand pets my cheek.
You remind me that
everything will be okay.

Just like the simple days –
swinging side by side on the playground,
using our imaginations in the forest.
Running wild and free.

Our adventures cut short
because I went away.
But then you went away for good
and now our chances are gone.

No more exploring the world together.
Our journey came to an end.
What life could've been like for you,
no one will ever know.

But here you are.
You came back to me,
waiting for the day I arrive
so we can be together again.

I finally notice your glasses are gone.
I guess you don't need them anymore.
But I still need you;
I never stopped needing you.

My only friend
with the power to make the bullies stop.
You were always a superhero –
my hero.

Immortalized in my brain,
that's where you are.
Not six feet under,
but in my heart and my dreams.

Butterfly Agony

I'm unable to focus.
The thoughts come and go
as they please.

Like butterflies fluttering around,
they're not in my stomach – they're in my mind.
Trapped,

destined to flap around
using every bit of strength
to keep from falling.

If they land and finally stop,
they'll lose all meaning.
They live to torture my brain, my memories.

Always following
their flight plan.
Why should they stop now,

when they can go on
haunting me, keeping my mind
in a constant state of agony?

The Wasp

The wasp enters through
a crack in the door.
Flittering and bobbing,
It disturbs me.

It zooms straight at me.
On guard!
Swatting it away,
I miss.

Always Watching

You don't see it,
but I do.

My eyes are wide open,
noticing every tiny detail
that you constantly miss.

Either you miss them because you don't care
or you're too afraid of what you might see
if you give it your full attention.

Me? I don't have a choice.
My gaze is attracted to the horrors,
like a magnet always pulling my head
in the direction of what I wish not to see.

The past.
The future.
The happiness.
The pain.

All of these combine
to form countless moments.
Moments to rejoice, reflect, or to fear.

Mostly just fear – of everything.
It's as if I'm sitting in a brainwashing chamber,
forced to watch the worst-case scenarios
play over and over in my head on the silver screen.

Of course it drives me crazy,
but I can't turn away.
What choice do I have?

The Scales

Bring me to existence.
I want to feel it.
The embrace of a loved one,
a dream achieved.

To exist and live,
what a joy that must be.
Loving and hoping and wishing,
being truly alive.

Why must there be pain,
no solace, no joy?
I'm trapped in this hourglass,
time slipping away.

Never achieving existence,
only going through the motions.
I'm not alive, I tell you;
I'm already dead.

Been this way for years.
Moments of defibrillation woke me briefly,
but those were rare.
They didn't go unnoticed, though.

Those moments just didn't outweigh the pain,
the constant sadness I feel,
consuming each part of me
every god damn day.

Unclear

I stick the key in,
never knowing what awaits on the other side.
Total darkness.

Faint shadows appear
but they deceive me.
Luminous aberrations dance in the dark.

I put one foot in,
like the hokey pokey.
Except my foot never comes back out.

Once I'm in, I'm in,
destined to be surrounded by the dark,
a shroud of nothing.

I manage to reach the light.
It allows me to see clearly;
I search around.

Dropping the burdens of the day,
I use my eyes to gaze.
I find myself in the process.

Center of Attention

Peripheral vision –
that part of my eyesight that betrays me
all day long.
Thinking someone, something is there.
But it never is.

Always making me second-guess,
turning my head,
looking around,
the crazy takes over.
I can't find what my brain tells me to look for.

Either I'm too distracted
or my brain is playing tricks on me.
Probably the latter, I'm sure.
The doctors would probably all agree,
but they don't see what I see.

A stranger spying,
an animal ready to strike.
A lurk here, a look there.
The all-seeing eyes of everyone and everything.
All eyes on me.

The Middle

There's no happy medium with my heart.
It's either guarded,
surrounded by deep metal
that no one can penetrate,

or it's wide-open
for everyone to see,
letting people in –
even strangers.

This makes me vulnerable,
easily attacked and outnumbered
by the forces
taking over my heart.

It weighs heavily,
as if a thousand set of feet
trample across my chest.
A never-ending stampede.

My fresh, raw wounds
attract the salt.
It stings.

A Formation of Atoms

Rising from the ashes,
the thoughts emerge.
Time to let it all out.
They creep in, stay, and release.

They rise and fall,
bringing out the best and worst in me
until I no longer know
which version of myself I am.

Constantly dying
inside and out.
My atoms accumulate
over and over.

Rebranding my identity
to better fit society,
trying to ignore
the construction of myself I hate.

Am I my own architect
or does my brain decide
which thoughts get in
and which emotion comes out?

Lack of control
allows the narrative to change.
My atoms rearrange once more.
I am born again.

The Curse of Being Born

The lights are too bright,
they give me a migraine.

My body collapses into the darkness.
Of course it does –

the dark has been pulling me ever since I was born.
Meant for the dark, the tragedy.

That's who I am,
the fucking card dealt to me.

A game I didn't want to play,
a game I never asked to be a part of.

I can't hold on to this card any longer.
Let it fall where it may.

I want it out of my hands,
no longer responsible.

Just let me leave the table.
Take all my chips.

Let the darkness take me.
I can't beat it.

Oh how I've tried,
I played my best game.

But it wasn't enough,
it was never going to be.

So I resign;
take me.

Let it be quick.

DEATH

Back & Forth

A spinning mind.
Countless scenarios creep in,
they knock down my walls.
Thoughts rush in as fast as they can.

A ceiling fan of worst-case scenarios
slaps me over and over.
And I'm torn.
Ripped to shreds.

Fright

A loud noise –
the lightning bolt enters my body.
I jump,
the shakes begin.

These strange rhythms –
out of place at first,
like me.
But soon they're put back in place.

As are we all,
put back into the universe.
Sometimes the way we came,
kicking and screaming with fright.

Side Effects

My stomach balloons.
The dizziness sets in.
Is this from the new pills?

Now I'm nervous,
must take a different pill
to calm me down.

The headache begins,
setting the groundwork
for a migraine and the nausea.

My mind's always in turmoil.
Why can't my body just rest?
Healthy, but hurting.

I can't think straight,
wincing at the pain,
the daily struggle.

Simply being human
is enough to bring me down.
Why am I alive?

Safe & Sound

I've not felt safe in years.
Safety implies a sense of security.

How secure can you be
once your life's been threatened?

Eyes always watching,
keeping track of my every move.

Being watched doesn't mean you're safe.
Instead, you're paralyzed –

never knowing which way to go
or where to turn, who to trust.

When the eyes stare, stare back.
Meet them halfway.

It's the only way
to prevent their attack.

Mixing Elements

Startled by the crashing of waves.
I knew they'd come,
I saw it so clearly.
But then it happened and I was afraid.

Scared of the noise,
apprehensive of the beauty.
Uncertain of where the water would stop,
counting all the possible scenarios.

My feet are wet now.
I contemplated too long.
Soon I'll be drowning,
head under water.

Trapped by the persistent thoughts
always dragging me down
to hell.
Through water cold and flame hot,

the volcano spits me out and I lay
just for a moment.
I'm content on the hardened lava surface,
soothed by both the cold and the warm.

An unsettling mixture,
here and before,
remembered and forgotten.
The earth moves back into place.

Yet I'm stuck,
sinking into the sand,
each piece between my toes.
Barefoot, awaiting my fate.

All the Elements

Drowning, but no water around me.
It's all inside – asking me to throw up
every bit of my insides.

The panic started.
It rushed to my thighs,
making them shake
like a willow in the wind.

Except I don't get the comfort
of weightlessly floating
in the cool breeze.

I'm hard and sturdy
like the Tin Man.
The tremors make my knees
clang together.

I'm a Scarecrow in a Tin Man body.
The panic sets my body on fire;
I burn as quickly as brush.

But I'm trapped inside the tin,
gasping for air,
feeling every ember
on my skin.

Fire and water mix,
forming a dangerous combination.
The fire makes me run
while the water keeps me grounded.

This tug of war is not unlike
the tug of war for my soul
many years ago.

Flashbacks

I watch from a distance
as it all falls apart.
Like a movie theater,
I'm in the back row
where I belong.

A permanent place for me,
the row to myself,
forced to watch the pain, the struggling.
It plays over and over;
rewind, fast forward.

A forced pause on the tragic, the trauma.
Skipping through the enjoyment,
memories fading by as I watch them go.
Destroyed and twisted into something they're not.
I want them back.

I need all the good memories –
they keep me safe.
A security blanket for me.
Without them, I freeze
and so do the tapes of my life.

It Remains

My lungs get heavy.
I breathe out.
I try to swim –
crying, grasping, searching.

The anxiety tortures me,
I tremble.
My body attacks itself,
I let the fear in.

Make no mistake,
my flaws show;
the open wounds will not heal –
the stitches rip open.

The pounding of my heart –
it startles me.
It awakens my soul and my dreams,
but they vanish into the night.

I close my eyes,
blood flows through my veins.
The chest pains start,
they ignite a spark in my soul.

I awaken.
I breathe.
But it's only temporary –
anxieties always come back.

Gasping for Death

People say you only die once.
The.
      Final.
            Decay.

But I don't see it that way.

We die.
Every.
      Single.
            Day.

In heartbreak. In sadness.
In those moments that take your breath away.

Not the moments when you hold your lover close and kiss them.
Nor the moment when a surprise dinner is waiting on the table.

It's the moment when your breath is taken away,
like when you fell off the jungle gym in 2nd grade
and landed straight
On.
      Your.
            Back.

When all you can do is gasp. Gasp for breath.
Gasp.
      For.
            Death.

Tragedies

Two suicides and an accidental.
Suffocation by pillow,
gun in the mouth,
rope around the neck.

All tragic.

All replaying in my head before I fall asleep.
No wonder the nightmares come.

Loud

You scream at me for no reason.
I buckle under the weight of your words.

Paralyzed by the fear that howls,
sending shockwaves through my body.

Panic.
        Ah, there it is.

Like heroin to my body,
it keeps me nervous. Yet, alive.

Stunned by my surroundings,
the voices get to me.

Despair.
        Oh, here it comes.

Falling

I have this dream;
I'm walking on a tight rope
viewing myself from a forced perspective.
Underneath.

Below me,
slightly in frame,
a fiery surface –
Hell.

Each night
I try to walk
across the right rope.
Trembling.

I can never quite
seem to make it across.
I always fall to my doom.
Shaking.

Take Me

A chill in the air.
I feel you
after all this time.
I guess you found me.

You were always on my mind,
haunting me in my nights,
causing chaos for my days,
and now you've come.

The day has finally arrived.
Take me with you,
cool me to my core.
I'm willing now.

Addicted

I've got to stop
doing this to myself.
It's breaking me further
when I'm trying to get fixed.

Like an alcoholic wanting more
or a druggie needing more,
here I am
longing for it again.

Not a buzz
or a high,
but the end all be all.
Death.

Always an Option

Knocked down by the wave of anxiety
that crashed into me.

Heart pounding.
Head hurting.
Body shaking.

I close my eyes,
wishing for a better moment.

No more pain.
No more sadness.
No more crying.

The madness has to stop,
every part of me wishes it.

I carry on.
I continue to live.
I hate it.

Loving those around me
while hating myself.

Love not found.
Despair consumes me.
Only loneliness lives here.

Forgive me
for I don't know what I'll do.

Cues

"Help me," I say.
It's up to you to listen.

    But do you?

        The echoes in the distance,
        the screams fading out.

"Help me," I say.
It's up to you to listen.

    But will you?

        The words aren't spoken,
        the thoughts are on my lips.

"Help me," I say.
It's up to you to listen.

    But can you?

        I can only speak with context clues
        and nonverbal cues.

"Help me," I say.
    But it's too late.

Tangled

He walked in on me,
well hung.

He dropped his things and ran to my side,
dead gaze.

He shook my body, trying to find life,
not home.

He removed the rope and laid me down gently,
no breath.

He performed CPR and pounded on my chest,
I awoke.

I'm still here. Always barely holding on.
By a thread. By a rope.

The Feeling

The depression has taken ahold of me again.
I'm physically forcing my body to sit
instead of
running for a sharp object
to inflict self-harm.

All I want is to release the pain
that comes on suddenly
without warning.
It hits me,
body trembling.

A unique twist on fight or flight,
fighting to sit on the couch.
Flying is out of the question.
I must remain
where I am.

So I stay glued to where I sit,
never moving.
Is it worth the risk of getting up?
Will I walk by the scissors
or will it be a kitchen knife this time?

Now I'm avoiding every fucking room of the house
just to stay alive.
Life is a god
damn trap.
We're never free until we are.

Bleeding

Stop the bleeding,
put the pressure on it.
Keep me alive
just a little longer.

Stop me from leaking,
pouring my soul out,
revealing secrets no one should know.
Or should they?

Stop the trembling
with those loving arms.
The ones that hold me close,
putting me at ease.

So many problems,
too many holes to plug.
The dam will break soon;
it will be the Great Flood.

The great flood of me –
sending me into the universe,
not knowing where I'll land
or who I'll meet on the way.

But if I'm with you,
that will make all the difference.
Along for the ride, both of us.
We can bleed for each other.

Sleep Paralysis

A raspy whisper
sits on top of me,
crushing my bones,
holding my body down.

I sink deeper into the bed,
my lungs collapsing,
ribs cracking,
crushed beneath the weight.

The weight of you and your whispers –
of me and my demons.
Together, intertwined,
sometimes I can't tell who is who.

But then the fear appears and there you are,
crushing my soul again.
Words leave me and I'm speechless –
a slave to your control.

I muster out a scream,
hands flailing about,
feeling for you
to see if you're really there.

Dark shadows seem to move,
confusing me further.
Real or not?
The whispering demon.

Crushing my soul
just for the hell of it.
One final exhale,
I scream.

Gravity

You pushed me to the floor;
gravity did the rest.

It joined you in the chaos,
applying pressure on me.

Gravity using its power,
the unwanted sensations.

Your body over me,
the carpet beneath me.

Bleeding,
Scratching,
Screaming.

Always clawing my way to the top.
Fighting gravity, fighting you.

In this moment,
I am changed.

Like wedding vows,
for better or worse.

And worse it is –
changed because of you.

But gravity holds no accountability
of my changed state.

I'm left alone
with my brokenness, with my memories.

Gravity keeps me stuck,
grounded in that defining moment.

To you

You weren't the only one.
There's another
far worse than you.
But you did what you did.

You're overshadowed and I don't think about you as often.

But now here you are,
being suggested by Facebook
to be my friend.
Something we can never be.

Someone who I have left far behind.

I quickly blocked you as fast as I could,
but not before I saw your face.
And now it's too late.
Flashbacks come pouring in.

I remember that night.

Here come the panic attacks,
tremors, and tears.
It's as if I'm experiencing it
all over again.

You. The other one. All the assaults.

Each one
lasting forever.
You've cost me
part of my life.

I'll never get back.

Calamities

Disasters,
one after the other,
coming and going.

Visiting me,
always wearing out
their welcome.

I pray for them to leave,
leave me be.
Leave me in peace,
not pieces.

But disasters don't enter smoothly –
they strike like a snake,
never knowing
who or what they will damage.

It's always me.
I'm the one hurt.
Venom for a victim.

Course Correction

The stream flows on,
muddy – no, bloody.
Filled with tears and memories
floating about.

Sinking deep,
spreading their disease.
Soon I'll have
a contagion on my hands.

Bathed in blood,
I take the leap.
Circling and spiraling,
away I go.

Pulled and torn,
pieces of me floating about.
Air can't find my lungs
because not a drop of me is left.

Bits & Pieces

One push and I'm gone.
Fragile.

Pick up the pieces of me.
Together.

Cracks so deep I'm scarred.
Broken.

Too many missing parts.
Forgotten.

Parts laying on the floor.
Scattered.

Sweep me up.
Trash.

Bathroom Floor

I fold like a chair onto the bathroom floor,
the cold tiles somehow warm my body.

The sensation startles me at first.
How can I be warm when I'm so cold?

Freezing to death,
hands like ice.

Try as I might,
there's still no end in sight.

No end for the loneliness.
No end for the madness.
No end for the sadness.

Only.
The.
End.

Flood

The floodgates open,
water washes over me.
I collapse,
lying in a puddle.
The reflection I see isn't clear,
but whose is anyway?

Another wave crashes down,
drenched from head to toe.
I awaken,
moving slightly this time.
Stuck in the same spot,
but who isn't?

The waves bury me this time,
too far down to come back up.
I inhale,
filling up my lungs with water.
The panic sets in and I regret,
but who wouldn't?

Cut

I cut myself today –
found a pair of scissors in the drawer.
One, two, three, four slashes –
enough to make a mark.

One almost started to bleed,
the others stayed still, skin unbroken.
I had enough sense to use cotton swabs.
It stung for a moment – the alcohol and peroxide.

What have I done?
Am I trying to leave a permanent mark?
Ashamed, I wore long sleeves to go out,
hiding the marks I hope do not turn to scars.

Maybe time will heal these wounds
unlike the others.

Fishing for Tears

I try not to cry,
but I do.
The tears alleviate a small part
of my burdens –

the pressure placed on me
by the world,
by myself.
I struggle for air.

I lay still,
mouth wide open,
as if expecting the final breath
to draw out of me.

One last part of myself gone,
released into the universe.
Casting my burdens out,
just like my tears.

Blemishes

The blemishes stain a blood red,
like fire out of control.
Raging hot,

it burns me.
Yet, I feel nothing –
numb to the pain.

It's not the fire I'm afraid of,
it's the cold –
that blistering wind that makes you bundle up in layer after layer.

The cold that stings like ice,
cuts like a knife,
and leaves you frozen and alone.

What happens when you play with fire and ice?
Can you tell the difference
or are you numb like me?

Do the two mix, forming a unique bond?
Or do they repel,
canceling each other out?

Hot and cold.
Fire and ice.
Life and death.

Reflect

You don't get to talk to me,
not ever again.

You're cut off,

like drinks at the bar.
Now it's time to sober up.

You're all alone,

think about what you've done
and who you've hurt.

You're beside yourself,

soak up the loneliness and regret.
You're filled with it.

You should be.

All of You & Me

I yell at you for nothing at all,
flipping the switch again
to my different personality.

Who am I?
All fits and rage,
filled with both anger and love.

The neediness sets in.
I know you hate it.
but I crave it; without it I'll die.

Here I am again,
sadness taking over
for no reason in particular.

Then comes the yelling again.
God, I'm tired of hearing myself –
it's exhausting.

It takes every breath
to be needy and sad,
to yell and be angry.

But it takes all of you to put me back together.
The puzzle with missing pieces,
scattered and hard to put together.

Let Your Conscience Be Your Guide

The middle ground
between asleep and awake,
the numbness of the body
not knowing which side to choose.

My brain makes the decisions around here,
always thinking and clouding my judgment,
possessed by scenarios and the voices.
A demonic Jiminy Cricket in my head,
twirling his cane and adjusting his hat.

If only he took residence on my shoulder
instead of burrowing himself inside my brain –
the worst place to be.
Emotions come and go so quickly here.

And you, you watch me struggle,
dangling on a string,
jerking me around,
your cane wrapped around my synapses,
your hat covering my feelings.

A cricket causing so much damage
simply by playing his tune,
a lullaby soft enough to make me sleepy,
yet too harsh, keeping me awake.

If I ever get the chance
to get you out of my head,
I'll take it in an instant.
There'll be no in-between sleep,
I'll be fully conscious.

When that happens,
there's no stopping me.
My power will be limitless
and I'll choose rest.

The Game

I roll my grief up
into a hard ball
to put in my pocket.

I go to the arcade
hoping to have a good time.
I never do.

It's never joy,
only the absence of it.

I play numerous games of ski ball,
rolling my grief up the ramp,
hoping to score some points for myself
by letting go.

But the ball always rolls back to me, unchanged.
Sometimes it might chip,
showing a small crack or two – an indention.

But the grief wants me
to hold on to it for some reason.

It's not clear why,
but all will be revealed
once I leave the arcade.

Our Collective Horror

If I die in my sleep,
just know I'm so sorry.
I would've loved to give
you a proper goodbye.

I can't help but think
how you'll react
when you find
my lifeless body.

Will you shake me,
try to bring my back?
Will you kiss me
one last time?

Will my body be so cold,
it won't feel real?
Will you cry, scream,
or collapse against the wall?

Will you fall to your knees,
your head in your hands?
Will you rush to the nearest bathroom,
vomiting at the sight?

A sight imprinted on your brain forever.

How will you tell my family?
How will they take it?
Will everyone fall apart without me?
Would I secretly want them to?

I don't want to be forgotten.

Would I want you to move on,
finding love with someone else,
spending twice or triple the amount of years with them
than you ever got to spend with me?

Is it selfish of me for thinking that?
Does true anguish ever go away?
Would everyone be left
with broken hearts and "what ifs?"

Would people online
still remember me
once my social media statuses
abruptly come to a halt?

Am I even important enough to be worth remembering? I hope.

I wish I could be here
to help you cope with my death.
I wish I could tell you it's okay,
I'll love you for eternity.

I wish I could let you know
if I had a choice to spend forever with you,
I would choose you
each and every time.

I wish I could tell you
I would be okay if you moved on with someone else,
but you know me
and my insecurities.

I'd feel that I wasn't loved.
I'd be jealous of all the years you had with them
that I didn't get to have.
I would feel replaceable.

But the thing is? I'm dead.

I won't be seeing any of that happen.
I won't be watching from a distance.
I won't be watching, seeing, or doing anything ever again.
I'm completely gone.

But for now, I'm still alive.
I know you love me.
I know that no one has ever made me feel
like you've made me feel.

I know that you've touched my life,
changed me forever.
And for now,
that's enough.

What happens after I die will happen.
But just know, that when I was alive,
I was content –
happy with you.

So don't have any regrets after I'm gone.
Don't worry about me.
Someone else is out there
needing your affection.

Your love is too beautiful to waste.

REBIRTH

Elastic Hearts

Time brought tragedy,
our hearts met within the empty spaces.

Always struggling to remain attached
as the world pulled on each end of
every
single
heartbeat.

Each beat is a cry for freedom,
a reach for justice,
an expression of authenticity.

Brave.
That's what we are.

With a thousand scars on our bodies and minds,
we continue to enter the battlefield.

Never knowing.
Always, never ever knowing.

Witnessing

Beat me with the Bible,
hit me over the head.

Those meaningless words
used to affect me,

but not anymore.

Use those verses against me,
slap them in my face.

Those irrelevant tales
filled with countless chapters,

are only folklore.

Impotent

I'm angry with you.
You.
    Know.
        What.
            You.
                Did.
Years of torment without justice,
decades of horrors without answers.
You.
    Used.
        To.
            Be.
            Real.
But I know the truth now,
how you were never really there.
You.
    Were.
        Never.
            My.
            God.
Only what others portrayed
and they were all wrong.
You.
    Remain.
        Nothing.
            To.
                Me.

Planting Prejudices

The seeds are planted,
buried deep within our skulls,
burrowing deeply as we sleep.

Once conscious, the seeds bloom –
the great awakening.
Blossoming into what we are,
what we'll become.

Then the pollen falls,
scattering like ash,
touching everything it sees,
spewing thoughts and covering others
no matter how much they sneeze.

Congestion at its finest,
like stand-still traffic,
our minds won't budge.
We want only to plant our own seeds,
the safe, familiar ones –
never thinking of others.

As the pollen spreads,
so does the disease,
corrupting the innocent of souls
who never asked for this.
The seeds take root,
taking over our mind and the others,
reaping what we sow.

Go Away

You show up at our door
begging for more love,
but we've run out long ago.
Or my husband has at least.

I still pity you,
all of you, even the dead ones,
for wasting
your relationship with him.

He gave you years of our life together
to please you,
but you didn't care.
Never did.

Now it's too late,
you're long gone.
In the form of a cease and desist,
each one of you ceases to exist.

Seeing You Again

I see you at the store
and I run away.
I hurry past, hiding behind aisles
so you won't find your prey.

But it's not me who should be scared,
my fight or flight has me prepared.

Do you know how much strength it takes
to even go out
when all I ever see
are nasty looks in the crowd?

People ready to judge,
their biases, they won't budge.

They don't see a human,
only a sinner.
But by no longer caring,
I'm the real winner.

So this time, I won't run and hide.
I won't say hi either, just simply walk by.

Forgotten

I almost took a pill for you,
decided you weren't worth it.

Not worth the pain you caused
or the resilience you gave
trying to control me,
mold me into something I wasn't.

I'm no clay
and you're definitely not the potter.
I stand alone,
sturdy as a rock.

You won't move me.
You're completely forgotten.

An Existential Hoard

It's a mess in here.
Look around,
there's not a single smile to be found.

Watch your step.
Memories are scattered about;
you can't find anything in this old house.

Happiness used to live here
before everything turned to hell.
Now this old house is just an empty shell –

remnants and pieces of what once was
can be seen piled up in the corner.
A life lived, belonging here no longer.

It scares you to go back
to the house of broken dreams
where everything is exactly how it seems.

Nothing's changed a bit, in fact.
The harshness in the air,
never leaving you relaxed.

Close the door
and walk away,
but never forget this day –

the day you finally survived
and moved on
from the place you once called home.

Burning Bridges

The bridge collapses,
triggered by an explosive.
A bomb of intolerance.

A waste of a match.
A waste of a life.
A waste of a parent.

You say it's not love,
unlovable us,
floating in the water below.

We hang tight to a single float.
Together, taken by the current,
washed away.

Waking up on an island,
damaged goods still surviving
on our own.

A creation of a pair.
A creation of two lives.
A creation of husbands.

Me Time

Running away from you,
stealing responsibilities and paths.
This road I'm on is scary.

You refuse to come along
and it's understandable,
you never acknowledged the horror.

So why would you now,
when the nights are heavy
and my heart breaks slowly?

Hard for you to see;
worse for me to live through.
So stay over there.

You only caused more harm anyway.
A hard pill to swallow,
but who's the one forced to take pills now?

Just another side effect
of being alive.
This is my life.

You're now uninvited,
spirited away,
lacking the courage.

I'm left to be brave on my own.
Never thought I could,
but I've been courageous all my life.

This is no different.
Whether I have cheerleaders in the stands
or I stand alone, I remain grounded in my place.

It doesn't matter where you are.
It only matters where I am.
I'm here – for myself.

Mirrors

The mirror of our soul reflects us,
showing us every part of ourselves.

But sometimes the light refracts,
shining a light on each imperfection.

Smash the mirror and look away.
Don't believe what it says.

You know your worth.
Don't believe a false version of yourself trying to betray you.

You

You make it look easy,
being alive.
Like a summer breeze,
it's as if you float through life
without a care,
content.

The Way We Walk

The way you glide across the room –
in charge, with a purpose,
always fulfilling your goal.

I envy your walk,
the confidence you carry.
Back, straight up, standing tall.

I stay hunched,
in need of a chiropractor to set me straight.
Prop me up, back to life.

But confidence can't be received,
I must give it to myself,
earning it from only me.

Standing tall feels uncomfortable at first.
It starts by letting the weight of the world go,
falling right off my shoulders like a magic trick.

Rising up to face a new day,
it's a new me,
standing tall and proud.

As Long as We Live

Life ever-lasting,
you sing to me your sweet song.
My cup runneth over.

Filled by your love,
the sweet kindness
bringing ecstasy to my soul.

My corporeal form desires it so,
a body broken and worn out.
You tie it together with a beautiful bow,
somehow unraveling the knots.

Blood clots cover me;
a dissection performed perfectly by you.
Life is a bloody mess,
but you make it worth it.

Body and soul, all for me.
The greatest gift ever given –
security and hope.
The things we cannot see.

Love

Holding on to you
was the tightest grip
I've ever known.

A firm grasp of love
never to die,
but to last forever.

Surrounded by your arms,
the peace flows into me freely.
I welcome it.

Our Bed

The bed, cozy and warm,
holds both of us
together in our purest form.
Dreaming together.

Hours beside one another,
so close and so far apart.
If only our dreams connected,
forming one journey as we explore.

At least our hearts connect,
forming one love
in the face of all adversity;
a tight rope, impenetrable.

Chained together willingly
without added weight.
Only our love, light as a feather,
soft as a mattress.

Tobacco Memories

Take me back,
all the moments we spent.
Every destination
awakened my soul, a part of me.

Longing for the next time,
waiting to be with you.
To be there,
it's impossible.

But I dream it.
It fuels my heart and simultaneously, my agony.
Knowing time is an illusion,
it stays in place while we spin on.

We burn out,
cigarettes sucked up dry,
each piece of tobacco a memory.
Gone, crushed into the ground.

Quick, light another one,
I need the fuel
to remember the memories, and you,
savoring every little thing.

Bottle

I put my message in the bottle for you,
knowing it might never be found.

But you were worth the risk,
you always were.

I hope when the bottle finds you,
if it does,

you'll see the words written
as if I were speaking them.

You'll instantly know my love
because the words will absorb into you

and you'll be filled with my love,
forever together.

Find the bottle,
keep me alive.

Blip

A blip in your timeline, that's all I'd be
if I ceased to exist and stopped being me.

Just a few short years together, that's all we'd have.
Within an instant, we'd be missing our other half.

If I went away and found no more reason,
you'd keep living, from season to season.

Leaves would change and so would you,
growing older, maybe more subdued.

I'd hope you'd find a way to carry on,
to keep on living, as if you belong.

Because, oh how you do – you belong here.
The earth needs you, for many more years.

It needs your presence, your grace,
the beautiful expressions on your face.

The way you light up when you're excited
and the way you love, undivided.

So why don't you stay, even if it means letting me go.
Because, my love, you're oh so precious and I want you to know.

Final Goodbye

It was wonderful loving you.
Each day was its own universe
we explored, however briefly.
Some worlds are scary, others we wanted to stay in forever.

But you were always the one. And loving you was wonderful.

The touch of the skin.
The furl of a brow.
A blink.

Our reality should be known to everyone.
A love story unforgotten.
Me and you – we'll be famous,
famously in love, with everyone remembering our names.

Our love matters. We matter.

Dance, Dance

They dance around the room
without a care,
clothes twirling about.
They don't realize they've got it all figured out.

This dance called life,
it makes a mess of ourselves.
We bend and we break,
never realizing what's at stake.

Our shattered pieces stop
when the song ends.
They fall to the ground,
without making a sound.

Our lives, our moments
flutter about like butterflies
blown into the wind,
never knowing where we end or where we begin.

Keep dancing and loving
even when your favorite songs stop.
You know the ones, the popular, the timeless.
Because one day you'll need to embrace the silence.

The Candle

A stolen light
surrounded by darkness;
it shines alone
never knowing
the day it will extinguish.

The black of night
taunts the one flicker,
bobbing and weaving around,
trying desperately to remain.

The day will soon come
when the flame builds or dies,
collapsing or expanding,
lighting or darkening the entire room.

Either way, though,
it will have made its mark
by continuing to light
or remaining dark.

String Me Along

These invisible strings –
do they pull us apart
or tie us together?

They pull, surely, on our hearts.
But is it enough?

Must a pull be necessary
for us to do what is right?

Shouldn't we just inherently know
that we're good?

These visible strings show
all the flaws.

My strings are in threads,
unraveling fast.

Piece by piece,
they slip away.

As they fall,
they make beautiful music.

Like strings on a harp,
falling into glory.

Not falling to pieces,
falling into peace.

Wings

I flew away.
You just missed me.
Oh, how I soared
high below the clouds,

never making it quite to the top.
But soar, I did.
Nevertheless, it wasn't enough.
My flight plan was pre-determined.

Wings tattered and worn,
weathered by countless storms.
Feathers cut and ripped,
attacked by life.

But fly I did,
as best as I could.
Up, up, up,
rain droplets pelted me as I flew.

Sometimes the wind carried me,
like magic, I floated along
never realizing
it was my own wings.

My own wings carried me.
Without fail, they brought me high
into the sky, up in the air.
It felt so free to be alive.

Colors

The colors, oh the colors –
how they change and melt into each other,
forming something new.
Leaving behind the old,
only a few stay in place.

Each color falls
slowly to their death.
Much like us, I suppose,
flat on the ground,
Destined to lie there.

We step on the colors.
They stick to our feet sometimes,
grasping at any last life they can find.
But we kick them off,
like they are but nothing.

The colors are mistreated and abused,
as if they're meaningless.
But they know
just how important they are
to so many.

They're content
knowing their worth,
understanding the fact
that one day
they will fall to their doom.

But they accept their fate,
enjoying their time while it lasts.
However brief that may be,
watching the seasons come and go.
The colors, oh the colors –

I am a color.

I Can Take It

Contemplating it again.
You know,
that sweet release.

Maybe a bit of pain at first,
but then forever gone.
No more hurt.

No more hope, either –
not for the ones left behind anyway.
Only pain for them.

It's like the pain trades places,
I carry it all alone now.
But afterwards, it will be scattered.

Each of you will have to share
the pain I carried by myself
for so long.

Is that selfish of me?
Longing for this transference,
flowing from me to all of you.

With my escape,
I condemn each of you to be
plagued by how I always feel.

So, I guess
it's better to hold on to the pain.
Maybe that's the brave thing to do.

You don't realize it,
but I'm the hero,
taking the pain for you.

I take it because I can,
as bad as it hurts.
Better me, than any of you.

Drifting

I drift off,
what a sweet release.
My body feels the energy as it leaves.
Gone, hiding away –

hiding in plain sight;
in the air, the touch of the skin,
with the leaves and plants.
I'm not gone, just dispersed –

spread out in a billion pieces,
floating into the world.
A traveler who can't sightsee,
only falling where I land.

It wants you to come along,
to appreciate the small things –
a ladybug, a ray of light,
the way the rain speckles on the ground.

Each drop of my energy can be soaked up,
breathed in and released back out.
I am one with the earth,
ashes and dust forming together.

Think of me in every drop, every crumb,
even the flap of a butterfly wing.
I'll be there, just not here.
All around you, all around the world.

ACKNOWLEDGEMENTS

For anyone who had a hand in helping me edit and promote this book.

For everyone who has ever had my back and for those who kept telling me to write.

For supportive teachers who taught me all I know.

For family who believed in me and for friends who gave me special memories along the way.

For Mom, Dad, Elijah, Mawmaw, Amy, and Matt, who each have a piece of my heart.

For Marina and Bonnie, who never stopped being with me.

And for my husband, Luke, who brought me out of the shadows and into the light.

I love you all.

ABOUT THE AUTHOR

Caleb Woods began writing at a young age, first to cope with bullying at school and later to soothe his depressing thoughts. Growing up in the small town of Pisgah, Alabama, he was surrounded by religion and found it increasingly difficult to reconcile his faith with his sexual orientation. Caleb was told he would spend an  eternity in hell for being gay – and he believed it. He was first officially diagnosed with PTSD in high school after his closest friend died unexpectedly. He moved away to college but ignored his symptoms and didn't seek help for his mental illness. After years of suffering silently, he began to accept his sexual orientation and eventually met his now husband, Luke.

Despite a happy marriage, Caleb continued to suffer with symptoms of PTSD. At their peak, the night terrors and panic attacks finally drove him to seek professional help. His doctor quickly confirmed that PTSD was the diagnosis and it wasn't something to be taken lightly. Today, Caleb receives treatment for PTSD, panic disorder, and depression by attending reoccurring therapy sessions.

Throughout these years, Caleb wrote poetry about his specific struggles surrounding mental illness and growing up gay in the Bible Belt. In his debut book, *Harnessing Darkness: Expressing Mental Illness Through Poetry*, Caleb reveals his most personal thoughts – some dark, some light, some suffering, some uplifting, but all existential.

Currently, Caleb lives with his husband in Birmingham, Alabama. He is a full-time writer, author, and poet who enjoys reading, traveling, playing board games, and collecting pop culture memorabilia. Learn more about Caleb and his work at: www.calebislost.com.

If you or someone you know is struggling, please visit the following websites:

National Alliance on Mental Illness

www.nami.org

American Foundation for Suicide Prevention

www.afsp.org

The Trevor Project

www.thetrevorproject.org

GLBT National Help Center

www.glbtnationalhelpcenter.org

National Suicide Prevention Lifeline

www.suicidepreventionlifeline.org

55267603R00073

Made in the USA
Middletown, DE
18 July 2019